DMT:

The Complete Simplified Beginners Introductory and Step-by-Step Guide to Making DMT, and its Full Effects

JOHN RIVERS

Copyright @2021

COPYRIGHT © 2021 JOHN RIVERS

All rights reserved. No parts of this book may be reproduced, transmitted in any form or by any means – mechanical, electronic, photocopy, recording or any other except for brief quotations in printed reviews, without prior permission of the publisher.

DISCLAIMER

I am not advocating for the usage of illegal drugs. Where DMT extraction is prohibited, I do not recommend using this approach. Outside of a legal or conventional framework, I do not support the usage of DMT. This advice is for the purpose of reducing harm.

Table of Contents

CHAPTER ONE 1
  INTRODUCTION......................1
CHAPTER TWO..........................7
  WHAT IS DMT?......................7
CHAPTER THREE 12
  SOURCES OF DMT................12
    Plants Containing DMT 14
      Chacruna (*Psychotria viridis*) 15
      Jurema (*Mimosa hostilis*) .17
      Yopo (*Anadenanthera peregrina* Seeds) 18
      Chaliponga (*Diplopterys cabrerana*) 19
      Acacia Plants 21
    Plants in the United States Containing DMT.................23
    Other plant sources of DMT are as follows: 25

Using DMT-Containing Plants 25

DMT in the Brain 28

CHAPTER FOUR 30

SIDE EFFECTS AND INTERACTIONS 30

Side Effects 30

Dangers (or Risks) Involved 31

Serotonin Syndrome Warning 33

Interactions 34

Addictiveness 36

Tolerance 36

Tips for Reducing the Risk of Harm 36

CHAPTER FIVE 40

GENERAL INFORMATION 40

Is DMT Same as Ayahuasca? 40

How it feels like 40

How it is consumed 42

How long it takes to Work...42

How long it lasts................43

CHAPTER SIX.........................44

EXTRACTING DMT FROM NARUTAL SOURCES..............44

Extraction Procedure..........45

CHAPTER SEVEN 82

SIMPLIFIED DMT EXTRACTION CHEMISTRY.........................82

A Quick Method 96

How to know the Purity of Extracted DMT.................100

Information on safety.......102

CHAPTER EIGHT 105

TAPPING INTO YOUR DMT NATURALLY 105

Summary 132

CHAPTER ONE

INTRODUCTION

There has been a decrease in ritual in recent times. The rites that once helped to cast an individual out of modern connections and place him in a field of epiphanies have devolved into mere form, betraying the inner energies that must express in some way. Shamen are aware of their own inner powers. They are aware of the overwhelming psychological experience that everyone will have if they are to finish their inward trek and fall into the unconscious. Any metaphysical realization a human may have about himself or his universe is centered on the psychological crisis. Many people are lost in the world, searching for what is only held within, without these powerful experiences, without the rituals that express the journey's message, and without shamen to indicate the way. Some may perceive chemically forcing such spiritual breakthrough as a way to avoid the challenges that are necessary to test each person wanting to understand the reality of their life. But, in today's culture, where does one go to find these self-testing opportunities or to be struck speechless by their own or the universe's natural beauty? For decades, shamen provided these opportunities to members of their community, assisting them in maintaining a healthy psychological balance between the known and the mystical. This skill is now available to you in one of many forms, DMT.

DMT is one of the most potent hallucinogens ever discovered. It's related to psilocybin and LSD. There are no drug tests that can detect the presence of DMT. DMT will not show up on any of the basic NIDA-5 drug tests (presently known as the

"SAMHSA-5") or any prolonged drug test. DMT is a naturally occurring substance that has been identified in abnormally high amounts in the bodily fluids of people with schizophrenia. DMT is nearly seldom sold through dealers, produced infrequently, and utilized infrequently. It can, however, be easily produced from common plant materials and has been utilized for hundreds of years in many forms. However, DMT is not a "social drug." Respect the substance and its enormous potential. This is not a drug for the inexperienced, nor is it recommended for people seeking a new "high." Few people seek out DMT-enabled visions, and even fewer people return to them. Even seasoned psychedelic users have had terrifying experiences with DMT on their first dose. Make sure you do your research to see if DMT is right for you. **I emphasize that learning more about this drug (and any other drugs you intend to use) will make you a better chemist, tripper, and guide**.

This guidebook is intended to serve as a quick reference for those who are new to extracting DMT. I'd want to urge others to contribute their own written insights to this guidebook. When attempting to make any of these goods, the reader is advised to read through the instructions numerous times in order to become well acquainted with the entire procedure. Please be aware that DMT is an illegal substance in the United States and is regulated by the federal government. The following information is provided solely for educational reasons.

CHAPTER TWO
WHAT IS DMT?

DMT, also known as N, N-dimethyltryptamine, is a hallucinogenic tryptamine substance (i.e. drug). This medication, also known as Dimitri, has effects that are similar to psychedelics like LSD and magic mushrooms.

It's also known by the following names:

- ✓ Fantasia
- ✓ 45-minute psychosis
- ✓ Businessman's trip

- ✓ Spiritual molecule
- ✓ Businessman's special

For good reason, DMT is regarded as "The Spirit Molecule." DMT is one of the most potent psychedelics known to man. It is found naturally in many plant species and is thought to be secreted in trace levels in mammalian brains. Although the subject is debatable, it's probable that natural DMT plays a role in out-of-body experiences or spiritual states.

DMT, like the other famous psychedelics LSD and psilocybin, is a chemical that mimics the neurotransmitter serotonin. The

5-HT2A receptor, which is predominantly found in areas of the brain involved with high-level cognition: self-awareness, emotions, and introspection, is responsible for DMT's psychological effects.

DMT produces a brief, intense psychedelic experience when smoked or injected intravenously. The sensation of being ripped from their bodies and flung across space at extraordinary speeds has been reported by users. DMT causes vivid visions and aural hallucinations of distant landscapes, secret dimensions, and godlike entities. It frequently causes users to engage in profound introspection, allowing them to review prior memories and gain a new perspective on life.

DMT can also be used in the form of ayahuasca, an ancient psychedelic drink consumed in traditional South American healing rites. This is a very different experience from smoked or injectable DMT, lasting several hours rather than minutes and frequently producing vomiting and diarrhea. Despite the awful sounding experience, ayahuasca has been linked to a number of therapeutic effects, including depression treatment.

In the United States, DMT is classified as a Schedule I controlled substance, making it unlawful to manufacture, buy, possess, or distribute it. Although it has lately been decriminalized in some cities, it remains unlawful under state and federal law.

CHAPTER THREE
SOURCES OF DMT

DMT is found naturally in a variety of plant species and has long been employed in religious rites in various South American countries.

Additionally, it can be synthesized in a laboratory.

Although DMT is outlawed everywhere, the legality of DMT-containing plants varies. DMT-containing plants can be ordered online in various areas.

You can cultivate your own DMT-containing plants from seeds if you're patient, as seeds aren't always as tightly regulated as plants. Reed Canary Grass seeds, for example, are available online in several regions.

DMT is found naturally in hundreds of plant species, but seldom in quantities big enough to cause psychedelic effects when consumed or smoked.

Pure DMT crystals, which can be smoked on their own or used to make pharmahuasca or changa, can be easily harvested from plants.

Depending on where you live, you can legally buy a variety of DMT-containing plants. Even in nations where DMT is outlawed, it is occasionally allowed to purchase plants containing DMT as long as they are not used to extract DMT or manufacture hallucinogenic compounds such as ayahuasca.

Keep in mind that DMT-containing plant laws can be complicated and opaque, and nations may choose to prosecute you for possessing one unless they have specifically stated that such plants are legal to possess.

Before acquiring plants that are a natural source of DMT, always verify your local laws.

Plants Containing DMT

Here are some of the most well-known DMT-producing plants, many of which, depending on where you live, can be acquired online. Check your local regulations; while you may be able to acquire these plants online and cultivate them at home, extracting DMT from them or preparing them for ingesting may be unlawful.

Chacruna *(Psychotria viridis)*

One of the most common admixtures in ayahuasca brews is

chacruna. *Psychotria viridis* is a large Amazonian shrub that is now grown throughout South and Central America. It produces huge green leaves with a significant amount of DMT (about 1% dried weight).

The leaves are traditionally placed in a boiling pot of *Banisteriopsis caapi* vines, and the liquid is reduced into a thick, dark liquid, resulting in one of the most popular types of ayahuasca. The psychedelic symbiosis created by the combination of DMT from *P. viridis* and MAOIs from *B. caapi* results in DMT staying in the body for longer than it would normally.

Traditional eye drops containing the liquid from fresh *P. viridis* leaves have been used to alleviate migraines and headaches.

Psychotria viridis dried leaves can be purchased online. DMT can be extracted from the leaves like you would any other DMT-containing plant if it is legal in your area.

Jurema *(Mimosa hostilis)*

This bushy tree, sometimes known as *Mimosa tenuiflora*, can reach a height of eight meters. Jurema is a plant native to Central and South America, and its root bark is used as both a medicinal and an entheogen.

The powdered bark is said to be a good pain reliever and is commonly applied to burns and wounds. It's also been used as an aphrodisiac and a general health tonic in the past.

Jurema's root bark contains about 1% DMT and is popular among DMT extractors because it's reasonably easy to come by in large quantities. Jurema is available for purchase online.

Yopo (*Anadenanthera peregrina* Seeds)

Anadenanthera peregrina is a South American tree that currently thrives in the Caribbean as well. The tree produces huge, dark brown seeds that contain DMT, 5-MeO-DMT, and bufotenine, which are hallucinogenic chemicals.

These yopo seeds were traditionally roasted and powdered into a powder (cohoba), which was then snorted in entheogenic ceremonies to induce a state of altered consciousness. Yopo is used by many different peoples throughout South America.

It's unknown whether yopo seeds can be used to extract DMT, and it's unlikely to yield as much as more common species like *M. hostilis* or *P. viridis*. If you're interested in yopo, it's probably best to make a snuff out of the seeds rather than trying to extract it.

Yopo seeds can be purchased on the internet.

Chaliponga (*Diplopterys cabrerana*)

Chaliponga, also known as chagropanga in Quechua, is a long vine that grows solely in the Amazon basin and is commonly used as an admixture in ayahuasca.

Chaliponga leaves contain a variety of hallucinogenic chemicals, including DMT (which accounts for around 1% of the dry weight), 5-MeO-DMT, bufotenine, and beta-carbolines.

Chaliponga may not be a suitable choice for DMT extraction due to the presence of other compounds in the leaves. It is, nevertheless, a common ingredient in some changa recipes since it can help to simulate an ayahuasca experience when used in a smoking blend. It can also be utilized in authentic ayahuasca preparations.

Acacia Plants

Acacia is a genus of plants that includes hundreds of species with a wide range of traditional and medical purposes. Acacia species, which can be trees or shrubs, are most typically found in Australia and Africa.

Acacia trees and shrubs are resistant to fire and provide a home and food supply for butterflies. Hundreds of species exist, each with its own appearance and biology — though they all have huge green blade-like leaves.

DMT is one of the hallucinogenic chemicals found in Acacia trees. Although not all Acacia species have been studied for DMT content, the following four have been found to contain considerable amounts of DMT (and occasionally additional alkaloids):

- *Acacia acuminata* – The bark and leaves contain approximately 1% DMT, although they also contain other alkaloids
- *Acacia confusa* – Its root bark of contains roughly 1% DMT
- *Acacia drepanolobium* has about 1% DMT in its leaves and bark
- *Acacia simplex* has 1 – 2% DMT in Its leaves and stem bark, however it also contains other alkaloids

Although additional alkaloids may be present in some Acacia species, anecdotal reports suggest that this does not interfere with standard DMT extractions, making these plants a good source of DMT.

Plants in the United States Containing DMT

DMT can be found in a variety of plants native to the United States.

- ✓ Bulbous Canary Grass (*Phalaris aquatica*) – Grows primarily in Californian grassland
- ✓ Reed Canary Grass (*Phalaris arundinacea*) – It is an

invasive species in North American wetlands
- ✓ *Desmanthus illinoensis* (Prairie Bundleflower) – This plant grows in Texas, Florida, Pennsylvania and North Dakota

The plants above are all natural sources of DMT.

Other plant sources of DMT are as follows:
- ✓ *Acacia maidenii* bark – Contains 0.36% DMT
- ✓ *Acacia simplicifolia* bark – Contains 0.86% DMT

- ✓ Virola shoots and flowers – Contains 0.44% DMT
- ✓ *Pilocarpus organensis* – Contains 1.06% 5-MeO-DMT
- ✓ *Phalaris tuberosa* – Contains 0.060% DMT

Using DMT-Containing Plants

The manner you employ DMT-containing plants will be determined by their unique characteristics! Some plants, such as yopo seeds, are probably best used as they have been for centuries. Others, such as chaliponga and *P. viridis*, are good ayahuasca brew ingredients. Chaliponga and *P. viridis* can both be used in changa dishes. Finally, plants like *M. hostilis* are excellent sources for extraction of DMT.

Unfortunately, without any form of preparation, consuming DMT-containing plants is unlikely to generate much of a psychoactive impact. This is due to the modest amounts of DMT present, as well as the fact that your body breaks down DMT quickly unless an MAOI is present. This is why DMT is extracted from these plants most frequently for usage in hallucinogenic concoctions.

DMT derived from plants can be smoked on its own or added to a changa recipe:

- ✓ When smoking pure DMT crystal on its own, the experience is exceedingly brief and can be rather intense. It also necessitates a more careful smoking approach, as well as, ideally, some additional equipment, to ensure that the crystal is not overheated (making an unpleasant taste and destroying the DMT). A bong or vaporizer is generally used for this

- ✓ To produce changa, simply dissolve the extracted DMT in a solvent and soak it into a plant mixture, which may then be smoked once totally dry. Changa can be consumed using a bong, pipe, or joints

DMT in the Brain

No one can be certain.

Some researchers believe it is produced in the brain by the pineal gland and released when we dream.

Others say it is released at the time of birth or death. Some even believe that the release of DMT upon death is to blame for those magical near-death experiences you hear about. Certain spiritual practices, such as breathwork, may elicit effects similar to those of a DMT trip!

CHAPTER FOUR
SIDE EFFECTS AND INTERACTIONS

Side Effects

DMT is a potent drug with a wide range of mental and bodily negative effects. Some of these are desirable, while others aren't.

DMT may have the following mental effects:

- ✓ Depersonalization
- ✓ Euphoria
- ✓ Changed perception of time
- ✓ Floating
- ✓ Vivid hallucinations

Keep in mind that some people's mental affects can last for days or weeks after they've used the drug.

The following are some of the physical effects of DMT:

- ✓ Rapid heart rate
- ✓ Agitation
- ✓ Increased blood pressure
- ✓ Paranoia
- ✓ Disruptions in vision
- ✓ Dilated pupils
- ✓ Nausea, or vomiting
- ✓ Dizziness
- ✓ Eye motions that are fast and rhythmic
- ✓ Stiffness or pain in the chest
- ✓ Diarrhea

Dangers (or Risks) Involved

There are dangers (or risks) involved, some of which could be dangerous.

The physical side effects of DMT, which include an increase in heart rate and blood pressure, might be dangerous, especially if you already have a heart disease or high blood pressure.

DMT consumption can also lead to:

- ✓ Seizures
- ✓ Confusion
- ✓ Loss of muscle coordination, increasing the risk of falling and injury

It has also been linked to coma and respiratory arrest.

DMT, like other hallucinogenic substances, has the potential to produce long-term psychosis and hallucinogen persistent perception disorder (HPPD). Both are uncommon, and are more likely to occur in those who have a history of mental illness.

Serotonin Syndrome Warning

High amounts of the neurotransmitter serotonin can be caused by DMT. This can result in a potentially fatal illness known as serotonin syndrome disorder.

DMT users who are also using antidepressants, particularly

monoamine oxidase inhibitors (MAOIs), are more likely to acquire this illness.

If you've used DMT and are experiencing the following symptoms, seek medical help right away:

- ✓ Confusion
- ✓ Muscle spasms
- ✓ Disorientation
- ✓ Muscle rigidity
- ✓ Irritability
- ✓ Hyperactive (or overactive) reflexes
- ✓ Tremors
- ✓ Shivering
- ✓ Pupils that are dilated

Interactions

DMT can interact with a variety of different medications, both prescription and over-the-counter, as well as other substances.

If you're using DMT, stay away from the following substances:

- ✓ Alcohol
- ✓ Amphetamines
- ✓ Antihistamines
- ✓ Cannabis
- ✓ LSD is also known as acid
- ✓ Opioids
- ✓ Mushrooms
- ✓ Benzodiazepines
- ✓ Cocaine
- ✓ Ketamine

✓ Gamma-hydroxybutyric acid (GHB), which is also known as liquid V and liquid G

Addictiveness

According to the National Institute on Drug Abuse, the jury is still out on whether DMT is addictive.

Tolerance

Tolerance refers to the necessity to use more of a medicine over time in order to attain the same results. According to 2013 studies, DMT does not appear to cause tolerance.

Tips for Reducing the Risk of Harm

DMT is incredibly potent, despite the fact that it is found naturally in a variety of plant species. If you do decide to try it, there are a few things you can do to lower your chances of having a negative reaction.

When consuming DMT, keep the following in mind:

1. **There is strength in numbers**: Don't rely solely on DMT. It's best to do it with individuals you can trust.

2. **Make a friend**: Make sure you have at least one sober

person on hand in case things go out of hand.

3. **Take note of your surroundings**: Make sure you utilize it in a secure and comfortable environment.

4. **Please take a seat**: To lessen the risk of falling or harm while tripping, sit or lie down.

5. **Maintain a straightforward approach**: Don't mix DMT with alcohol or other substances.

6. **Choose the appropriate time**: DMT's effects

can be rather powerful. As a result, it's ideal to use it while you're already feeling good.

7. **Know when it's time to skip it**: If you're on antidepressants, have a heart condition, or already have high blood pressure, stay away from DMT.

CHAPTER FIVE
GENERAL INFORMATION

Is DMT Same as Ayahuasca?

Almost. Ayahuasca's primary active element is DMT.

Traditionally, ayahuasca has been made using two plants known as *Banisteriopsis caapi* and *Psychotria viridis*. The latter contains DMT, whilst the former contains MAOIs, which inhibit the breakdown of DMT by particular enzymes in your body.

How it feels like

As is the case with most medicines, DMT can have a wide variety of effects on individuals. Certain individuals genuinely love the experience. Others find it terrifying or overwhelming.

In terms of psychedelic effects, users have described feeling as though they are speeding through a tunnel of dazzling lights and forms. Others report having an out-of-body experience and transforming into something else.

Additionally, some claim to have visited other worlds and communicated with elf-like beings.

Additionally, some individuals describe a quite severe comedown following DMT, which leaves them feeling uncomfortable.

How it is consumed

Synthetic DMT is often a white, crystalline powder. It is typically smoked in a pipe, but can also be vaporized, injected, or snorted.

When plants and vines are employed in religious rites, they are boiled to create a tea-like beverage with varied degrees of potency.

How long it takes to Work

Synthetic DMT acts quickly, with symptoms manifesting within 5 to 10 minutes.

Plant-based brews typically take between 20 and 60 minutes to take effect.

How long it lasts

The intensity and duration of a DMT trip are determined by various factors, including the following:

- ✓ How much of it you consume
- ✓ The way you use it

- ✓ Whether you've taken any additional medications
- ✓ Whether you've eaten

DMT's effects last approximately 30 to 45 minutes when inhaled, snorted, or injected.

Consuming it in a brew similar to ayahuasca can cause a two – six-hour trance.

CHAPTER SIX
EXTRACTING DMT FROM NARUTAL SOURCES

To begin, we must choose a plant that has the compounds we wish to extract. None of these plants are banned, and they grow wild and freely around the planet (much less can be said for some of our other favorite plants). The majority of these plant materials can be obtained online. A little study may find a significant amount of usable plant material growing nearby. Each plant's alkaloid concentration varies according to its growing conditions. Specific information about these plants and how to grow them is beyond the scope of this text, although it is readily available.

Extraction Procedure

For this experiment, we will use *Mimosa hostilis* root-bark to obtain a very pure form of NN-DMT free of 5-MeO-DMT or 5-OH-harmful DMT's side effects. We shall use common naphtha as a solvent. Additionally, notes on chemical adaptations and other variations of this process are included.

The following is a material list:

- *Mimosa hostilis* root bark (30g recommended starting quantity)
- Muratic acid (swimming pool acid)
- pH papers (litmus papers)
- Lye (Red Devil Brand)
- Naphtha (Zippo lighter fluid)

- ✓ Coffee filters and cotton swabs/cloth
- ✓ Funnel
- ✓ 3 labelled glass jars with lids, preferably sturdy canning jars, but pickle jars would suffice, labelled Jar A, Jar B, and Jar C
- ✓ Dish for evaporation (glass baking pan)
- ✓ Glass pipette (turkey baster)
- ✓ Gloves and goggles
- ✓ Distilled water

NOTE:

It is beneficial to test all non-glass materials with solvents to ensure that no undesirable reactions occur.

HAZARD STATEMENTS

- ✓ *Methylene Chloride*: Cancer risk is suspected. Cancer risk is dependent on the duration and intensity of interaction. If consumed, this substance is poisonous. Irritating to the skin and eyes. Irritates the respiratory tract. Blood cells may be harmed. It is possible that this will have an effect on the central nervous system. May result in blindness. Refrain from inhaling vapors or mist.

Take care when handling. Bear these dangers in mind if you substitute DCM for another solvent
- ✓ *Muratic Acid*

Step-by-Step Instructions

Step 1: Preparation of Plant Material

Finely grind the plant material. The finer the material, the higher the yields. The most effective method for pulverizing and rupturing the cell structure of any plant material is to repeatedly freeze and thaw it. *Phalaris arundinacea*, a robust and limber grass, is an example of a plant that requires this treatment. The root bark of *Mimosa hostilis* is easily pulverized in a blender to a fine powder, emitting a pink haze.

I. Freeze the grass cuttings overnight.

II. Using a blender, remove them and place the frozen clippings in it. While the clippings are frozen, attempt to liquefy them as much as possible

III. For optimal results, repeat this procedure of freezing, thawing, and blending with the plant material multiple times

Step 2: Acidify Water to a pH of 2

Wash two pickle jars, about 20 ounces each, in the dishwasher to aid in sterilization and cleaning. The jars should be labelled A and B. Fill Jar A halfway (i.e. $2/3$ way) with distilled water (15 ounces or 500ml preferably filtered). Pour into Jar A, ½ teaspoon (2ml) acid. Conduct a pH test on the water in Jar A. The pH of the water should be 2 or more. If not, dilute with additional distilled water (5% acidity).

NOTE:

Acid is produced in a variety of ways: Acid should always be added to water, not water to acid. To avoid adulterants, use distilled water.

- ✓ Distilled white vinegar (5% acidity, 2 cups or 500ml for 50g root-bark) or lemon juice
- ✓ Muratic acid is a type of acid that can be acquired at a pool store (10ml 30 percent HCl to 1 liter water is recommended)
- ✓ Hydrochloric and sulphuric acid of reagent grade (overpoweringly potent without dilution.)

To Jar B, add powdered root bark.

LABORATORY NOTES:

Proper pH paper testing technique: Swirl the acidic solution using a glass stirring rod (or something that will not corrode in the acid). Lightly dab the pH paper with the stirring rod. To conserve pH paper, clip only a little portion of the strip for each test. If a pH meter or pH sheets are not available, certain organic sources produce antocyanines, which change color when exposed to a variety of pH values. A reasonable indication of the pH range can be obtained using red beats or red cabbage. This is not always the best course of action, but it works. Blend or crush either red beats or red cabbage to generate the indicator solution. Using a strainer, separate the juice from the pulp and discard any residual plant matter. If insufficient pigment is discovered, try extracting additional pigment from the mushy pulp using water. If the solution has an excessive amount of pigment, simply dilute it with water. Although the indicator solution generated has a limited shelf life, it can be refrigerated for several weeks. For reference, the following is a crude pH chart: (*litmus document includes a pH chart*)

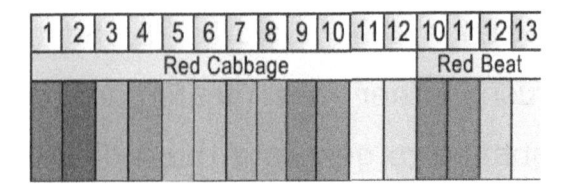

1	2	3	4	5	6	7	8	9	10	11	12	10	11	12	13
Red Cabbage												Red Beat			

Step 3: Convert Alkaloids to Salts

Transfer sufficient acidified water from Jar A to Jar B using a pipette (or turkey baster) to cover the root bark at the bottom of Jar B (8 ounces, or 250ml acidified water into Jar B). When the acid combines with the root bark, the alkaloids (elf-spice) are converted to salts. To aid in this process, we can:

I. Shake the contents of the jar on a regular basis. This increases the amount of root-bark that comes into touch with the acid.

II. The acid's strength dictates the length of time it should be heated (the weaker it is the longer time it should be heated and vice versa). Allow no evaporation of the liquid contained within. Avoid boiling. Maintain a temperature of less than 50° C (122° F). Due to the fact that we are utilizing pickle jars rather than Pyrex, they can easily shatter if heated or cooled too quickly. To reheat the solution, it is advisable to use a double boiler filled with hot (not boiling) water. Simply turn off the heat source and let the solution to cool to room temperature gradually.

1. Heat the jar for 15-30 minutes when using Muratic acid.

2. When using weaker acids, the contents should be simmered overnight.

Allow 24 hours in order for the contents of the jar to react for the first time. The alkaloids (tryptamines) are transformed to salts, which are then soluble in water. The aqueous solution now contains our elf-spice.

Step 4: Filtration

Using cotton balls or cotton cloth, plug the funnel's bottom to form a cotton filter. Through the funnel, pour the contents of Jar B into Jar C. Squeeze the contents of the root-bark filter to extract any remaining juices. Reintroduce the root-bark that was captured by the filter into Jar B.

LABORATORY NOTES

When straining material through a cotton-filter or a coffee filter, it's best to filter the thinner components of the solution first, then the mushy and bulkier components, which can clog the pores of your filters. The higher the filtering efficiency, the faster and more efficient your emulsions will be, resulting in a cleaner output. Cotton must be utilized specifically. Other fibers may react with our solvents. A tea strainer (wire strainer) is a convenient tool for separating large ruffage. A vacuum filter is another approach to improve this process. There are various types, the most affordable of which is a water vacuum filter that connects to a standard household faucet. These are really convenient, helpful, and effective.

Step 5: Collect 3 Extractions

Rep Steps 2, 3, and 4 two more times. The first extraction is critical. Allow the contents of the jar additional time to react during the final two extractions for optimal results. Shake Jar B four times daily for one week, each time sifting through a cotton-filter. Each time, collect the acidic contents in Jar C. Clean Jar A and Jar B after the initial three cotton-filtration cycles and discard any leftover root-bark.

After completing all three extraction stages, re-filter the contents of Jar C using a paper coffee filter rather than a cotton filter.

I. In the bottom of the funnel, place many paper filters (coffee filters).

II. Strain the contents of Jar C into Jar B using the paper filters.

III. Once completed, clean Jar C.

Rep this procedure as necessary to remove as many particles as possible from our solution.

LABORATORY NOTES

The majority of the alkaloids we are looking for will change to salts during the initial extraction process. The second and third extraction steps take longer. This will ensure that we extract the maximum amount of alkaloids feasible from our material. The third phase can be shortened to 1 – 2 days, but yields will suffer. Bear in mind that these are all rough estimates.

Step 6:   Defatting

Following that, we defat the solution. This is normal laboratory practice when extracting alkaloids of this type. This technique removes oils, lipids, and other undesirable components from our aqueous solution, while significantly increasing yields. Other DMT salts are insoluble in non-polar solvents, except for DMT acetate, that is soluble in non-polar solvents such as chloroform and DCM (these are chlorinated non-polar solvents). Therefore, when using white vinegar like your acid, you need to defat with naphtha or ether because chloroform or DCM is extracting DMT acetate together with oils and fats, undermining the objective of this step. While this procedure is not necessary when utilizing *Mimosa hostilis* root bark, it is strongly suggested when using any plant material with chlorophyll-containing leaf.

This is accomplished by diluting the acidic solution with an organic (non-polar) solvent. Prior to employing any solvents, evaporate a considerable amount (500ml) of the solvent in a dish. This ensures that no leftovers or orders remain after evaporation is complete (commonly found in many over-the-counter solvents). This solvent will be evaporated, leaving a smokable form of DMT, later in this guide (Step 10). Whatever your solvent adds to the end result, you may be smoking it. Several further non-polar organic solvents are listed below.

I. **Naphtha**

Coleman fuel, VM&P naphtha, Zippo, or lighter fluid are all acceptable substitutes. If you are unclear of the impurities, evaporate a tiny amount in a dish and inspect the residue. If warm naphtha is utilized for the extraction phase rather than the defatting phase, it will extract alkaloids considerably more effectively than cold naphtha. Naphtha is thought to be more selective than DCM at capturing these alkaloids. Naphtha climbs to the jar's rim.

II. **Methylene Chloride**

Additionally referred to as DCM or dichloromethane. Frequently used as an acrylic adhesive solvent. Pure DCM is available in craft stores. Prior to using DCM, all non-flammable paint strippers must be distilled (they contain a paste that holds several unwanted substances). Additionally, the paint stripper may contain methanol (most marine grade paint strippers are 80 – 90 percent DCM). Methanol is an organic solvent as well. DCM distils at a temperature of 41° C or 106° F. The purest DCM is preferred. Could result in cancer and blindness. Precautions should be taken. Methylene chloride sinks to the jar's bottom.

III. **Ether**

Contained in automotive store-bought engine-starting fluid. Spray the contents of an engine-starting aerosol can down a 12 inch (30cm) piece of ¾ inch PVC pipe to eliminate the liquid ether. While the ether condenses on the pipe's walls and falls into the jar, the inert propellant is released into the air. Ether is a highly volatile asset. Ether floats to the jar's rim.

IV. **Chloroform**

Chloroform (CH_2C_{12}) can be acquired online from arts and crafts supply warehouses. It is corrosive to organics and has a boiling point of 35 – 65°C (95 – 149° F). Chloroform sinks to the jar's bottom.

It is critical to keep track of the type of organic solvent you are using. We shall employ naphtha in our defatting procedure.

Add 50 – 100ml (2 – 3½ ounces) naphtha to Jar B. (Approximately 10 – 15% of the volume of our acidic solution is sufficient naphtha for this step. Determine what 10% of the solution's total volume is and add that amount of naphtha to the jar). Cap Jar B and vigorously shake the contents for 20 minutes. Allow the emulsion (foam, bubbles, solutions, particles, etc.) to split into two distinct layers by setting Jar B aside (much like oil and water will separate). This could take up to 24 hours (48 in some cases). Oils and fats travel to the non-polar solvent layer, leaving our alkaloids in aqueous solution. Because we are employing naphtha, the solvent layer in Jar B will rise to the top. Remove and discard the solvent layer using a pipette (or turkey baster).

Repeat the defatting process twice more.

LABORATORY NOTES

A separatory funnel comes in help when it comes to splitting and eliminating layers of solution. This apparatus is made up of a single chamber with a tapering bottom. A closed faucet is located at the bottom. The container is then filled halfway with the two solutions and mixed. The equipment is then left aside until the two fluids split into two distinct layers. The lower portion of the fluids can be emptied via the bottom faucet and stored or discarded in a container. Fill a

Ziplock plastic baggie halfway with your concoctions and hang it from one corner to create a rapid separatory funnel. Once the layers have separated, the bag's bottom corner is squeezed and then cut to allow for drainage. It is recommended that you test the baggie to ensure that your solvents do not melt it.

Step 7: Preparation for Basification

Using a common organic non-polar solvent, we shall prepare the solution for the alkaloids migration in this stage. We shall utilize heated naphtha as our solvent (other solvents are identified in Step 6 above).

Add 100ml (3 ounces) heated naphtha to Jar B. Shake the jar vigorously for five minutes.

Step 8: Basify to a pH of 9

Now it's time for the solution to be basified. This "unhooks" the salt and converts the alkaloid to its "free base" form. The alkaloids will no longer be a salt and will no longer be water soluble. This enables us to extract them with the addition of the organic solvent in Step 7. Normally, ammonium hydroxide is used; however, for this experiment, we will use sodium hydroxide

(NaOH), which is found in household lye crystals (Red Devil drain cleaning) and is readily accessible at hardware stores. Lye is extremely caustic and has a tendency to react violently. Take the necessary precautions when working with lye.

5g (0.2 ounces) lye and 95g (3 ounces) distilled water make an excellent basifying solution. We dilute the base to avoid localized pH increases that would damage the alkaloids in the area where the concentrated base is being added. Assemble the following basic mixture:

I. Fill Jar A 95ml (3 oz.) to the brim with water.

II. Add 5g (1 teaspoon) lye to water gradually. Shake and fully mix contents.

III. Ascertain that the pH is 12 by performing a test.

Transfer little volumes of solution from Jar A to Jar B using a pipette.

I. After each transfer of lye solution, stir and monitor the pH of the contents in Jar B until the solution reaches a pH of 9 – 11.

II. Shake the jar vigorously but be cautious of the pressure that may build up inside. Frequently remove the lid and vent! As the alkaloids are converted from acid salts to free base, the solution will turn gray. It may have the consistency of a thick gel. As you add more base, the solution will darken and become slick. Throughout this process, the jar will heat up.

You have now synthesized the non-polar soluble free base alkaloids. DMT has a pKa (natural pH) of 8.68 according to the Merck Index (making this the ideal pH to extract at). In numerous studies, the average pH of the final basified solution in Step 8 was 10, which consistently produced acceptable results.

Step 9:   Emulsions

An emulsion will form as the alkaloids dissolve in the non-polar solvent supplied in Step 7. The strength of the emulsion created is related to the force with which it is stirred. Heavy, quick churning results in a thick emulsion that can take up to four days to settle. Light, slow stirring over a prolonged length of time results in an emulsion that separates swiftly while maintaining yield. Allow the emulsion to split into two different layers overnight in the container. If the emulsion hasn't cleared after 48 hours, try these steps:

I. Adding a lot of salt and gently swirling can help with emulsions by making the polar layer more polar.

II. Increase the amount of organic solvent.

III. Filter the solutions several times more via a cotton filter. A paper filter isn't going to cut it.

IV. Check the pH and raise it.

V. The solvent layer will usually have a small hue to it, but it may also appear completely transparent in some situations. Simply evaporate a small amount in a glass dish to conduct an early test of your extraction. The residue should have a synthetic odor (a smell like plastic). This odor is a characteristic of your tryptamine.

The naphtha will separate into a thick orange/pink emulsion with tiny bubbles, which can take up to 48 hours. Always wait a few days before attempting to break down the emulsion using other methods. Keeping the naphtha heated during each extraction will increase the amount of alkaloids it contains. To assist in keeping the jar warm, place it in a saucepan of warm water. Naphtha is a floater. If we utilize DCM as our extraction solvent in Step 7, we will obtain a more rapidly resolving emulsion than if we use naphtha, less than an hour in some situations. The solvent may darken significantly, usually just to a reddish-brown or yellow tinge. DCM is a sink. Allow at least 24 hours for the contents of the jar to completely react. Allow a minimum of 4 days for reactions to complete at room temperature if employing methanol.

Remove the matching solvent layer from Jar B with a pipette and store it in Jar A.

Step 10: Extraction and Evaporation of the Final Alkaloid

Step 7 and Step 9, in that order, should be repeated twice more. Our elf-spice falls into our solvent from the basified aqueous solution.

Jar A should now contain the combined solvent fractions from our solvent extractions. Fill a glass baking dish halfway with the contents of Jar A. Allow the solvent to evaporate before proceeding. It could take up to a week for the water to evaporate (depending on your solvent). Keep the dish with the solvent away from heat or an open flame during this period.

Depending on how carefully you followed the technique, the residual substance could look like anything from a sticky orangish sludge to white or pale-orange crystals. Using a razor, scrape the material from the baking pan. A suitable starting dose is about 25mg (try about the size of a pea). From 30g of *Mimosa hostilis* root-bark, you might generate 5 – 6 doses (275mg) assuming optimal yields. The smell will indicate whether DMT is included in the final product. DMT has a synthetic odor, similar to that of some produced polymers.

LABORATORY NOTES

Your product may contain trace levels of hydroxide after the DCM has evaporated. Some people find hydroxide in the final product to be unpleasant. Try soaking the DMT crystals in water and allowing the water evaporate to help decrease this. To aid in the removal of hydroxide, water can be introduced to the solvent evaporating dish.

CHAPTER SEVEN
SIMPLIFIED DMT
EXTRACTION CHEMISTRY

Because *Mimosa hostilis* root bark is the most often acquired DMT source, this DMT extraction guide is specifically for it. It's commonly comes in the form of a coarse powder.

Although this method is for *M. hostilis*, it should work with any DMT-containing organic material;

you just need to adjust the amount of beginning material to the amount of DMT found in the plant species you're using.

The most popular method is known as an 'acid/base extraction,' although it's quite difficult. I'll walk you through the 'straight to base' extraction method, which is a little less difficult. A synopsis of the chemistry is as follows:

Your DMT-rich plant is powdered and combined with a base, most often sodium hydroxide (NaOH). The plant substance is dissolved, leaving DMT molecules floating around in a base solution.

The following step is to extract the DMT from the base solution. Fortunately, there is a simple answer: the base solution is charged (polar), but the DMT molecules aren't (non-polar). This means that by introducing a non-polar solvent to the polar base solution, the DMT molecules will be attracted out. This non-polar solvent (which now contains the DMT) separates from the rest and creates a distinct layer from the base solution.

The DMT molecules must next be extracted from the non-polar solvent, which can be done via evaporation or freezing.

Step-by-Step Instructions

Please read the guide thoroughly and make certain you understand it before attempting the process.

Ingredients

- Plant containing DMT such as *Mimosa hostilis* root bark
- Water
- Lye (granulated sodium hydroxide)
- Vinegar (for cleaning up Lye spills safely)
- Naphtha VM&P. However, if it unavailable, it can be substituted with 40 – 60 Petroleum Ether

EQUIPMENT

- ✓ Personal protection is provided by a fume mask, safety goggles, and rubber gloves
- ✓ A blender or grinder that can smash ice is required
- ✓ Glass mixing jar (about a litre or more) with a wide opening and a tight-fitting lid (depending on how much plant material you are starting with)
- ✓ 4 collection jars with lids (glass jelly/jam jars will suffice)
- ✓ Coffee filters
- ✓ A spatula made of rubber

- ✓ Freezer
- ✓ Pipette
- ✓ Eyedropper

Step 1: Extracting DMT from the Plant

I. Wear a mask to avoid breathing in the powder as you cut and combine the plant material until it's as fine as you can get it.

II. Slowly add a spoonful of lye to the water in your mixing jar, stirring until dissolved. To create 50g *Mimosa hostilis* bark, combine 750ml water and 50g lye. ***NOTE: Lye is a chemical that can cause chemical*** *burns and should be handled with caution. Vinegar may be used to clean up any spills. Wear gloves and eye protection.*

III. Add the powdered plant to the jar, shut it tightly, shake it well, and set it aside for approximately an hour.

Step 2: Extracting DMT from the Base Solution

I. Pour 50ml naphtha into the mixing jar for every 50g *Mimosa hostilis* bark.

II. Replace the lid on the mixing jar and slowly stir for approximately a minute, turning it over a few times. Don't shake it since shaking it will make it difficult to separate the two layers afterwards.

III. Allow the two layers to separate by setting your mixing jar down.

IV. Repeat the gentle agitation process a few times more.

V. Once the layers have separated following your final agitation, use your pipette to transfer the top (clear) layer to one of your collecting jars. This is the location of your DMT. Avoid taking any of the darker, bottom layer, as it contains harmful bacteria that you don't want to spread.

VI. To obtain every last bit of DMT out of the base solution, add more naphtha to the mixing jar and repeat the previous processes three more times.

V. Optional: keep the last batch of naphtha in the mixing jar for a few days to extract the most DMT from the base solution.

VI. Place all four of your collection jars (which contain DMT in a naphtha solution) in the freezer for at least an hour.

Step 3: Extracting DMT from the Naphtha Solution

I. Your DMT should have crystallized in your collection jars thanks to the freezer. To collect the DMT, strain the solutions using a coffee filter. The naphtha can be preserved and used again in the future.

II. ***NOTE:*** *According to numerous people, DMT*

crystals are not visible after freezing. They may be suspended in the naphtha and appear after the naphtha has been poured through the filters. However, if your freezer isn't cold enough, the crystals may take longer to form. To get a cooler temperature, you can leave your collection jars in the freezer for longer.

III. Get every last drop of naphtha solution out of the collection jars using your rubber spatula.

IV. Lay your coffee filters out to dry with care. After drying, this DMT powder is ready to smoke, but it can be further refined in the optional step below.

V. Many people discover that their DMT remains adhered to the jars' sides; if there are no crystals on your coffee filters, look inside the jars for them.

Step 4: DMT Recrystallisation for Future Refinement (Optional)

I. Fill a small glass jar halfway with DMT powder.

II. Put your solvent (naphtha or heptane) in a different glass jar. For every gram of DMT powder, you'll need roughly 25ml of solvent.

III. To heat up the contents of both glass containers, carefully place them in a pan of hot water. ***NOTE: Because the solvent produces flammable vapors, DO NOT use a gas burner or keep open flames nearby***.

IV. Add a few drops of your heated solvent to the DMT powder with an eyedropper. Continue to swirl the glass container and add solvent until all of the DMT is dissolved. If you can, use as little solvent as possible.

V. Take the pan off the heat and allow it cool to room temperature.

VI. Place the glass jar containing the dissolved DMT powder, which is now at room temperature, in the refrigerator.

VII. Place the container in the freezer for a few hours when it has cooled down.

VIII. You can now use a coffee filter to filter out your

purified DMT crystal. This procedure can be repeated to achieve even higher levels of purity.

A Quick Method

If you don't want to bother with all of those procedures and just want to get your DMT out of your plant as soon as possible (without bothering about purity or yield), here's a simplified method:

Ingredients

- ✓ Plant containing DMT such as *Mimosa hostilis* root bark
- ✓ Water
- ✓ Lye (granulated sodium hydroxide)

- ✓ Vinegar (for cleaning up Lye spills safely)
- ✓ Naphtha VM&P. However, if it unavailable, it can be substituted with 40 – 60 Petroleum Ether

Equipment

- ✓ Personal protection: rubber gloves and safety goggles
- ✓ Large mixing bowl made of ceramic (5L)
- ✓ Masher for potatoes
- ✓ A large measuring jug (2L)
- ✓ Large baking dish made of glass
- ✓ Fan

Procedure

I. In a mixing dish, break up 400 – 500g of *Mimosa hostilis* root bark. Make sure the bark doesn't fill more than half of the dish.

II. Slowly pour 200 grams of lye into 2 – 3 liters of water. ***NOTE: Lye is a chemical that can cause chemical burns and should be handled with caution. Vinegar may be used to clean up any spills. Wear gloves and eye protection***.

III. In the mixing basin containing the root bark,

pour your lye solution. Give it an hour.

IV. For 20 – 30 minutes, mix and crush your root bark using a potato masher.

V. Mix for another 20 – 30 minutes with 250ml of naphtha in the basin.

VI. Allow for a few minutes for the solvent to rise to the top of the mixture.

VII. Remove the clear solvent layer on top and pour it into your glass baking dish. Avoid getting any of the dish's lower, darker layer.

VIII. By blowing air across the baking dish with your fan, you can evaporate the solvent.

IX. The remaining powder is your DMT that can be smoked.

How to know the Purity of Extracted DMT

When you produce your own DMT, all you have to worry about is how well you followed the instructions. You may wind up with additional contaminants in your DMT powder if you employed low-quality ingredients or did a sloppy job (i.e. accidentally carried over some of the base solution). Smoking this can be rather uncomfortable.

There is a misconception that the color of DMT powder indicates its purity; however, the color of DMT powder is affected by a number of circumstances. It is generally safe to smoke powder that is white, yellow, red, or brown in color. If it's green or blue, it means something went wrong during the extraction process, and you should try again.

NOTE:

Many extraction techniques, as previously indicated, involve an acid/base extraction process, which we haven't addressed here because the straight-to-base method is much easier. However, there is a vast number of tutorials on DMT extraction, which you can research, if you want to be absolutely thorough and try an acid/base extraction.

Information on safety

In most countries, DMT is prohibited. I don't believe in breaking the law or utilizing DMT in ways that aren't legal or customary. If you do decide to use DMT, do your homework on the effects and risks.

DMT is a potent psychedelic that must be used with caution. You should be aware of the best ways to prepare for and integrate a psychedelic experience.

Keep track of how much you're taking! A 15mg dose of smoked DMT powder is recommended for first-time users.

Before you begin using these extraction guides, be sure you understand the process. Make sure you understand the changes if you're utilizing a DMT-containing plant other than *Mimosa hostilis* and alter your technique accordingly. If you're grinding up plant debris, wear rubber gloves, safety goggles, and a dust mask.

Avoid getting lye (sodium hydroxide) on your skin and always use safety goggles when working with it. If you get it on your skin, wash it off with plenty of water (and, ideally, vinegar to neutralize the lye if it's available). If it gets into your eye, flush it out with tap water for at least 20 minutes before seeing a doctor. If you spill a lot of it, use vinegar to neutralize it before cleaning it up. When adding lye to water, start gently and thoroughly mix it in.

CHAPTER EIGHT
TAPPING INTO YOUR DMT NATURALLY

For decades, seasoned meditators and breathwork practitioners have claimed to be able to "get high on their own supply."

However, scientists have consistently refuted this assertion, citing the usual argument that your body does not manufacture enough DMT to cause psychedelic effects (25 mg).

That's why the new research included in the DMT Quest documentary is so intriguing: it could explain what some people, and even our forefathers, have always suspected by employing methods that:

- ✓ Increase the circulation of cerebrospinal fluid; or
- ✓ Induce brain states that produce high amounts of gamma waves; or
- ✓ Activate the pineal gland or other regions of the brain; or
- ✓ Reduce the activity of MAO, the enzyme that degrades DMT

We might be able to get "high on our own supply."

So, if you're scared of exogenous DMT (and you should be), but still want to learn more about the impacts and benefits of a DMT-like state, here are some suggestions and tactics to help you tap into your own DMT naturally—while staying well within the law's bounds.

Step 1: Improve the Pineal Gland's Health and Function

As previously stated, research has partially confirmed Strassman's hypothesis from the 1990s that DMT is produced in the pineal gland — though we now know it isn't the only source of DMT in the body, as evidenced by a 2019 study in which rats were still able to produce DMT after their pineal glands were removed.

Regardless, the pineal gland has long been associated with spiritual awareness, creativity, dream states, and out-of-body or near-death experiences, and has been referred to as the "Seat of the Soul" or the "Third Eye."

So, until proven otherwise, I'm still inclined to believe that the pineal gland is linked to endogenous DMT in some way.

The pineal gland can now become calcified (calcium phosphate crystals build up) as a result of modern living, which is caused, at least in part, by environmental contaminants such as fluoride, other heavy metals, or pesticides.

Rapid aging, brain problems, neurodegenerative illness, cognitive loss, and psychiatric symptoms have all been linked to pineal gland calcification. Melatonin, a potent anti-aging hormone that regulates hundreds of activities including your vital sleep-wake cycles, is also produced by the pineal gland, and a lack of melatonin could be a cause in certain illness states.

On the same vein, calcium build-up may inhibit your brain's ability to manufacture DMT, implying that persons with a calcified pineal gland won't necessarily get as much benefit from a plant medicine journey.

While this notion has yet to be verified, taking steps to protect the health of your pineal gland will certainly increase your ability to more easily tap into brain states conducive to DMT release (and, if not, you'll be taking care of your precious brain at the very least).

Here are some tips for maintaining and improving your pineal gland.

Fluoride should be avoided

Fluoride is most likely one of the main causes of calcification in the pineal gland. It's been proven that the more fluoride in the human pineal gland, the more calcium accumulates. A 2019 rodent study indicated that rats on a fluoride-free diet had greater favorable growth of the pineal gland than rats fed fluoride-containing food and water.

As a result, if you want to keep your "Third Eye" in tip-top shape (as well as boost the health of everything from your hormones to your thyroid), do everything you can to remove fluoride from your environment, particularly your drinking water. At the very least, invest in a high-quality water filter that removes fluoride, use fluoride-free toothpaste, and stay away from non-stick pans and cookware.

Detox your Pineal Glands

The following meals and supplements are included in the plan to encourage detoxification, minimize calcification, and restore the function of the pineal gland, in addition to removing dangerous environmental chemicals like fluoride:

1. Iodine, which can assist the body eliminate heavy metals like fluoride by chelating them.

2. Shilajit, an adaptogenic Ayurvedic plant high in antioxidants and the strong binders fulvic acid and humic acid (or pure fulvic acid can just be taken).

3. Turmeric or Curcumin, which has been demonstrated to reduce fluoride neurotoxicity.

4. In addition to additional supplemental Vitamin A and Vitamin D$_3$, Activator X (a mixture of Vitamins K2, D, and A) can be consumed in the form of concentrated butter oil or ghee.

5. Chaga mushrooms, which contain high quantities of Superoxide Dismutase, a powerful antioxidant.

6. Raw cacao is thought to "stimulate the Third Eye" while also promoting blood flow and cleansing.

7. Tamarinds are edible fruit pods from a tropical African tree that have been found

in many tests to help the body excrete fluoride.

8. Raw apple cider vinegar, containing malic acid, a chelating substance that binds to heavy metals.

9. Chlorella or Spirulina, which contain high levels of chlorophyll, a well-known chelator.

10. Boron or boric acid, which has been demonstrated to be an "antidote" to fluoride.

You might also want to include organic oregano oil extract and beetroot powder to your list, as well as the tactics and approaches listed below for complete pineal gland support.

Peptides

Epitalon and Pinealon are two peptides that are recognized to maintain the health of your pineal gland.

Epitalon is a synthetic peptide that aims to mimic the natural peptide epithalamin found in the pineal gland. Epitalon has been shown in scores of animal and clinical tests to not only decalcify and restore the integrity of the pineal gland, but also to greatly reduce the risk of all-cause mortality and even to prolong telomeres, making it a potent anti-aging peptide.

Pinealon is a peptide that can help your pineal gland and perhaps boost your memory. Pinealon was found to enhance serotonin expression in the brain cortex in one study, suggesting that it may also stimulate other serotonin-related chemicals like DMT. It's recommended to take a dose of Pinealon prior to embarking on a journey of self-discovery with something like DMT to guarantee the pineal gland is functioning optimally and your body and mind are prepared to receive the full benefit of the experience.

BioCharger ("Pineal Gland Mastery" Mode)

BioCharger combines four different energy sources into one ultimate biohacking machine: light, voltage, frequencies & harmonics, and pulsed electromagnetic fields (PEMFs).

The BioCharger device has a mode called "Pineal Mastery" that releases energy levels that are supposed to activate your pineal gland and reduce concerns like calcification.

The BioCharger may possibly be able to improve your body's ability to manufacture endogenous DMT by targeting the pineal gland. This gadget has DMT-like effects, such as an uplift in mood, an increase in creativity, and an improvement in the ability to enter deeper flow states during work, meditation, or breathwork.

So, rather than taking a microdose of DMT or other psychedelics when you need a boost of creativity or attention, you may turn on the BioCharger to "Pineal Mastery" and meditate, breathe, or even bounce on a trampoline while absorbing its mind-enhancing energy.

Now, those were just ways to improve the health and function of the pineal gland, which, if you believe DMT is created in part by the pineal gland, should all help to boost your body's natural ability to induce DMT endogenously.

There are, however, procedures that can directly boost DMT production and, when used in precise ways or with specific tactics, can make you "higher" than you've ever been on any drug.

Step 2: Stimulate Endogenous DMT using Natural Methods

While it is not yet understood how, when, or why DMT is produced in the body, there are three tried-and-true methods that have been used for thousands of years as part of ancient spiritual traditions, cleansing ceremonies, and even in tandem with psychedelic rituals as a way to tap into "alternate brain states" — which are now known may be due to their ability to stimulate production of endogenous DMT are:

- ✓ Breathwork
- ✓ Meditation
- ✓ Fasting

Here's how to use these science- and history-backed techniques to naturally tap into DMT and have similar mind-altering, life-changing, perspective-shifting experiences as a full-fledged psychedelic trip.

Breathwork

Breathing practices can create naturally high levels of DMT.

Furthermore, the effects of "holotropic breathwork" are similar to those of LSD: a fusion of the left and right hemispheres of the brain, a combination of creative and analytical thought, and a large release of DMT and nitric oxide.

While the processes for how breathing practices may promote DMT production are unknown, there are a few theories:

Breathing Exercises Boost Gamma Wave Activity

Scientists did a baseline EEG test on someone practicing breathwork near the end of the DMT Quest documentary and discovered enhanced gamma wave activity in the brain comparable to DMT and 5-MeO-DMT.

Breathworks Promotes Cerebrospinal Fluid Flow

Outside of the brain, the cerebrospinal fluid contains some of the highest levels of DMT. The circulation of cerebrospinal fluid throughout the brain is controlled by respiration (breathing), according to a 2017 study. As a result, by focusing on breathing in a precise way, you may be able to increase DMT dispersion throughout the brain and body.

Breathwork Alters the Body's CO_2 and O_2 Ratios

Hyperventilation is caused by rapid breathing for an extended period of time, which results in an increase in carbon dioxide and a reduction in oxygen. Breathwork's capacity to create altered states of consciousness akin to DMT is attributed to lower oxygen levels, whereas it is attributed to increased CO_2 by some others.

Whatever the method, holotropic breathwork can put you in the "highest" condition you'll ever be (without the use of psychedelics), resulting in a powerful out-of-body experience unlike anything you've ever had before.

You can also microdose with a little psilocybin, hop in your sauna, and do Soma Holotropic Breathwork 1 – 2 times a month.

TIP

To activate your pineal gland before a breathwork session, dab a drop of Blue Lotus Extract or Third Eye from Essential Oil Wizardry on your top lip. If you really want a DMT-like experience, snuff powdered rapé with a Kuripe pipe before conducting breathwork.

Meditation

For thousands of years, experienced meditators have claimed to be able to induce altered states of consciousness similar to psychedelics through meditation alone.

In fact, when psychedelic use became popular in the 1960s, meditators frequently chastised users of drugs like DMT, accusing them of "cheating" the arduous labor of meditation.

DMT and other psychedelics tend to have similar effects to meditation in that they both appear to lower activity in the Default Mode Network of the brain (DMN).

The hippocampus, posterior cingulate cortex, and prefrontal cortex make up the DMN, which is important for daily processing, planning, strategizing, and reflecting. It's really beneficial to being a considerate, productive, and useful human being.

However, if the DMN is always active, we are unable to think outside of ourselves, cease worrying or ruminating, or exhibit creativity. Unsurprisingly, an overactive DMN is linked to greater instances of depression.

The ability to "switch off" the DMN is one of the benefits of psychedelic drugs -- and, coincidentally, regular meditation. This is thought to be the cause of high-dose plant medicine's "ego dissolving" effects.

Researchers identified similar activity in the DMN between those using psychedelics (LSD, psilocybin, and ayahuasca) and those in profound meditative states in a 2018 study that examined brain scans. This could mean that certain types of meditation, like high-dose DMT, have ego-dissolving, awareness-enhancing, and other transformational benefits.

It's feasible to achieve a mental state that rivals any external psychedelic substance by using any of the longer meditation approaches.

Instead of going on a third, fourth, or fifth ayahuasca retreat, some people may benefit more from committing to a strong meditation practice, which allows them to up-regulate their natural production of DMT while also reaping the many other advantages connected with meditation.

Alternatively, if you simply want to ramp up the effects, consider microdosing with DMT or psilocybin before your next meditation session.

You can readily research the dozens of different types of meditation methods.

Fasting for a Long Time

If you've ever done an extended fast, you probably saw a considerable rise in your attitude, energy levels, and productivity around the third or fourth day following a few days of painful suffering (aptly called as "The Suck").

While some believe that the euphoric benefits of fasting are due to your body switching to ketones for fuel, it's also possible that it's due to increased DMT levels, which are created by downregulating the activity of the enzyme that breaks it down: MAO.

In rats, prolonged fasting (three days) resulted in a 50% drop in MAO activity, according to a 2009 study.

Furthermore, if DMT works in the same way as other neurotransmitters like serotonin, tryptophan, or melatonin, another study found that fasting boosted levels of these substances all over the body, particularly in the brain and stomach tissue.

To put it another way, prolonged fasting appears to lower MAO activity, potentially resulting in larger quantities of endogenous DMT circulating throughout the body. This could possibly explain some of the cognitive, emotional, neuroprotective, and therapeutic effects linked with fasting, based on what we know about DMT's benefits.

You can learn about fasting, its benefits, and how to do it safely by doing some research.

Summary

DMT isn't only a recreational drug. It's a potent chemical that's found in far bigger concentrations in your body than previously thought, on par with other critical neurotransmitters. Additionally, without using any exogenous hallucinogens, it may be feasible to enhance your endogenous DMT levels and have similar benefits to a transformational psychedelic excursion.

Breathwork, meditation, and fasting, when combined with current ways to optimize and activate your pineal gland, may all have the ability to boost your natural DMT levels, allowing you to access a state of consciousness not normally available in ordinary life.

So, instead of inhaling DMT from a vape pen and falling into a 20 –

40 minute trance, a "natural DMT adventure" would look like this:

1. A dose of Epitalon or Pinealon followed by 20 – 30 minutes of holotropic breathwork.

2. Before a long meditation session, a few drops of Blue Lotus Extract or Third Eye from Essential Oil Wizardry on the top lip.

3. Snuffing a bit of powdered rapé or Zen spray before sitting in front of the BioCharger set to "Pineal Gland Mastery" mode.

4. Or 3 – 4 weeks of "pineal gland cleanse" followed by a 3 – 5 day prolong fast.

While these techniques are likely to improve your ability to manufacture and release endogenous DMT, the compound's exact function remains unknown.

Whether it allows us to enter a different spiritual realm where we can communicate with powerful entities or it permits us to enter a higher mental state, allowing us to perform superhuman acts or simply induces anthropomorphic data-driven hallucinations with no discernible reason, no one is aware. Yet.

And, while we don't have all the answers just yet, the recent renaissance of psychedelic research is encouraging, and it may just add to psychedelics' general adoption as a therapeutic tool.

Because, as science is beginning to show, these plant compounds are not only entirely natural to our bodies when taken responsibly, in the proper place, and for a reason, but they may also help us nurture a stronger sense of joy, connection, purpose, and love for our fellow brothers and sisters.

And one of the most important things we can accomplish in this life is to love one another.

Made in the USA
Columbia, SC
03 September 2024